THE BEST 50
SALAD DRESSINGS

Stacey Printz

BRISTOL PUBLISHING ENTERPRISES
San Leandro, California

Printed in the United States of America.

ISBN 1-55867-211-7
Cover design: Frank J. Paredes
Cover photography: John A. Benson
Food styling: Susan Massey

SALAD DRESSINGS FOR EVERY OCCASION

For many of us, the quest for the perfect bottled salad dressing goes unrewarded. Unfortunately, bottled dressings never seem to capture the taste and freshness of the dressings prepared in fine restaurants. This book will end your search.

In the following pages, you'll find new and interesting salad dressing recipes as well as tasty versions of the classics. The recipes are easy enough to whip up after a long workday, yet worthy of serving at your finest dinner parties.

Salads are a common addition to many people's menus, whether as a main course or as a side dish. As popular as salads are, however, many people are under the mistaken belief that the dressings are time-consuming and difficult to make. In reality, most dressings take only five minutes to prepare and can make a world of difference in the flavor of your salad.

The dressings in this book will add just the right amount of flavor to your crisp greens, crunchy red peppers or vine-ripened tomatoes. There are dozens of different tastes and textures. You will find dressings to suit any type of lettuce or vegetable as well as dressings that can be used as marinades or stir-fry sauces. In addition, look for a selection of fat-free dressings. Many of the recipes feature bonus ideas for making appetizers, side dishes and entrées. With this collection, you can make salad dressings for every occasion.

A WORD ABOUT GREENS

For the recipes in this book, you can use an array of possible greens. Suggestions for greens follow every recipe and are based on the consistency, flavor and style of the dressing.

For example, sturdy romaine lettuce is suggested for many of the heavier-bodied dressings, while tender butter lettuce is offered as the option for lighter, sweeter vinaigrettes. Most grocers are happy to answer questions that you might have regarding any of the more unusual varieties of greens that are listed.

BASIC INGREDIENTS

Following is a list of ingredients that are useful to have on hand when preparing salad dressings.

- canola or vegetable oil
- olive oil
- Dijon-style mustard
- balsamic vinegar
- distilled white vinegar
- cider vinegar
- white wine vinegar
- red wine vinegar
- seasoned rice vinegar
- garlic
- lemon
- honey
- sugar
- salt and pepper

SALAD DRESSINGS FOR EVERY OCCASION

ITALIAN BUTTERMILK DRESSING

If you do not have Italian herb seasoning, substitute ¼ tsp. dried oregano, ¼ tsp. dried parsley and ½ tsp. dried thyme. This is a fairly thin dressing. If you prefer a thicker consistency, use less vinegar.

¼ cup buttermilk
⅓ cup light or regular sour cream
¼ cup olive oil
¼ cup white wine vinegar
1 tsp. dried Italian herb seasoning
½ tsp. granulated garlic
¼ tsp. freshly ground pepper
¼ tsp. salt

CREAMY-STYLE SALAD DRESSINGS

Combine all ingredients in a jar and shake vigorously until smooth. Chill for at least 1 hour to blend flavors. Makes 1¼ cups.

Serving suggestions: Serve on romaine or red leaf lettuce, or on mixed greens. Toss with mushrooms, tomato, onion, cauliflower, green beans, olives, croutons, sprouts and/or garbanzo beans.

Create an appetizer: Sour Cream Vegetable Dip

Omit buttermilk and increase sour cream to ¾ cup. Reduce wine vinegar to ⅛ cup. Serve with crisp, cold vegetable pieces. Makes 1¼ cups.

YOGURT DILL DRESSING

This versatile dressing is great year-round.

½ cup nonfat or low-fat plain yogurt
¼ cup canola oil
2 tbs. light or regular mayonnaise
¼ cup white wine vinegar
1 tbs. water
½ tbs. fresh lemon juice
½ tsp. Dijon-style mustard
½ tsp. dried dill weed
½ tsp. sugar
¼ tsp. onion powder

Combine all ingredients in a jar and shake vigorously until smooth. Makes 1½ cups.

Serving suggestions: Serve on green leaf or oak leaf lettuce. Toss with cucumber and/or tomato.

Create an appetizer: Yogurt-Dill Vegetable Dip
Omit oil, vinegar and water. Serve with crisp, cold vegetable pieces.

Create an entrée: Poached Salmon with Yogurt-Dill Sauce
For a nice luncheon dish, serve dressing drizzled over cold poached salmon.

Create a side dish: Steamed Vegetables with Yogurt-Dill Sauce
Drizzle dressing over chilled steamed vegetables, such as asparagus or green beans.

CREAMY-STYLE SALAD DRESSINGS

POPPY SEED DRESSING

This is sure to be a crowd pleaser. The tangy onion-poppy seed combination is delicious.

½ cup vegetable or canola oil
½ cup chopped onion
¼ cup distilled white vinegar
1 tbs. regular or light sour cream

1 tbs. fresh lemon juice
2 tsp. sugar
½ tsp. dry mustard
½-¾ tsp. poppy seeds

Process all ingredients with a blender or food processor until almost smooth. Makes 1½ cups.

Serving suggestions: Serve on red leaf, green leaf, oak leaf, iceberg or butter lettuce. Toss with tomato, mushrooms, green beans, beets, croutons and/or sunflower kernels.

CAPER DRESSING

This is a great alternative to a Ceasar salad. The capers are a snappy change of pace

¼ cup canola or vegetable oil
¼ cup olive oil
¼ cup distilled white vinegar
2 tbs. finely chopped capers
½ tbs. caper brine
2 tbs. grated Parmesan cheese

2-3 tbs. lemon juice
1-2 tbs. light or regular mayonnaise
½ tsp. dry mustard
1 small clove garlic, finely minced
salt and pepper to taste

Combine all ingredients in a jar and shake vigorously until smooth. Chill for at least 1 hour to blend flavors. Makes 1 cup.

Serving suggestions: Serve on romaine lettuce. Toss with croutons and shaved hard cheese, such as Parmesan or Romano.

CURRY DRESSING

This out-of-the-ordinary dressing will spice up an everyday salad. For garnish, toss dried currants, coconut and peanuts with the salad. Or, serve the garnishes in small bowls on the side and let people sprinkle on their own.

½ cup nonfat plain yogurt
¼ cup seasoned rice vinegar
¼ cup vegetable or canola oil
2 tbs. white wine vinegar
¼ tsp. curry powder
⅛ tsp. ground allspice
⅛ tsp. ground ginger
dash chili powder

Combine all ingredients in a jar and shake vigorously until smooth. Makes 1 cup.

CREAMY-STYLE SALAD DRESSINGS

Serving suggestions: Serve on green leaf or red leaf lettuce, or spinach. Toss with cucumber, red pepper, jicama, carrot, raisins or dried currants, coconut and/or peanuts.

Create an entrée: Curried Chicken or Shrimp

Marinate chicken or shrimp in dressing for 6 to 24 hours before sautéing or grilling. Serve over rice with extra dressing as a sauce (do not use dressing that was used for marinating).

AVOCADO DRESSING

This is a thick dressing, but it coats well when tossed thoroughly with greens.

1 ripe Hass avocado, roughly chopped

¼ cup lemon juice

2-3 tbs. water

1 tbs. vegetable or canola oil

1 tbs. seasoned rice vinegar

1 small clove garlic, crushed

1 tsp. light or regular soy sauce

½ tsp. freshly ground pepper

Process all ingredients with a blender or food processor until smooth. Makes 1 cup.

Serving suggestions: Serve on green leaf, red leaf or romaine lettuce. Toss with corn kernels, tomato, onion, red or yellow bell pepper and/or croutons.

Create an entrée: Grilled Southwestern-Style Fish

Serve dressing as a sauce over seared or grilled ahi tuna, shark or swordfish. Accompany with a spoonful of corn kernels and a spoonful of chopped tomatoes or salsa. Serve as is or on a bed of greens that have been tossed with dressing.

CREAMY-STYLE SALAD DRESSINGS

EGGLESS CAESAR DRESSING

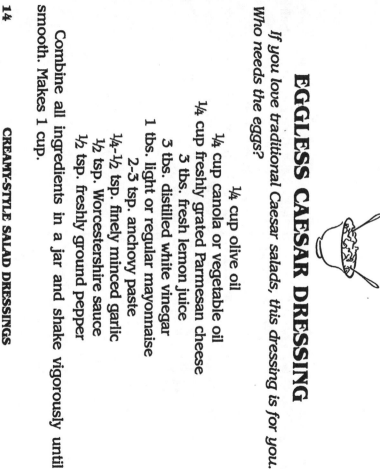

*If you love traditional Caesar salads, this dressing is for you.
Who needs the eggs?*

¼ cup olive oil
¼ cup canola or vegetable oil
¼ cup freshly grated Parmesan cheese
3 tbs. fresh lemon juice
3 tbs. distilled white vinegar
1 tbs. light or regular mayonnaise
2-3 tsp. anchovy paste
¼-½ tsp. finely minced garlic
½ tsp. Worcestershire sauce
½ tsp. freshly ground pepper

Combine all ingredients in a jar and shake vigorously until smooth. Makes 1 cup.

CREAMY-STYLE SALAD DRESSINGS

Serving suggestions: Serve on romaine lettuce. Toss with shaved Parmesan cheese and *Garlic Croutons.*

GARLIC CROUTONS

These make a tasty addition to salads of all types.

2 cups stale bread cubes
½ tbs. olive oil
1 tbs. butter, melted
1 clove finely minced garlic
1 tbs. finely grated Parmesan cheese

Heat broiler. In a large bowl, toss bread cubes with olive oil, butter and garlic. Add Parmesan cheese and toss again. Transfer cubes to a foil-lined baking sheet and broil until cubes are well browned on all sides, turning as needed. Cool completely before using. Add to tossed salad just before serving. Makes 2 cups.

CREAMY-STYLE SALAD DRESSINGS

SUN-DRIED TOMATO CAESAR DRESSING

Here's a new twist on the classic Caesar dressing. It is well worth the slightly long preparation time. Don't forget to add at least 1/4 cup additional grated Parmesan cheese to your salad.

1 large egg yolk*

1 tbs. grainy Dijon-style mustard

1 tbs. (heaping) anchovy paste

3½ tbs. balsamic vinegar

2½ tbs. lemon juice

2-3 cloves garlic, finely minced

10 oil-packed sun-dried tomatoes, finely chopped

½ cup olive oil

¾ cup vegetable oil

1½ tsp. dried thyme

salt and freshly ground pepper to taste

CREAMY-STYLE SALAD DRESSINGS

Place egg yolk, mustard, anchovy paste, balsamic vinegar, lemon juice and garlic in a jar and shake vigorously until smooth. Add sun-dried tomatoes, olive oil, vegetable oil, dried thyme, salt and pepper and shake well. Chill for at least 1 hour to blend flavors. Makes 2 cups.

Serving suggestions: Serve on romaine lettuce. Toss with shaved Parmesan cheese, avocado and/or *Garlic Croutons,* page 15.

* Some health authorities discourage using raw eggs in salad dressings due to a minimal risk of contamination.

CREAMY-STYLE SALAD DRESSINGS

17

CREAMY ROASTED GARLIC DRESSING

The rich flavor of this dressing adds interest to any meal. Try it over roasted or grilled vegetables, such as eggplant, zucchini, onion and bell pepper.

1 bulb garlic
3 tbs. olive oil, plus more for drizzling
3 tbs. balsamic vinegar
1 tbs. distilled white vinegar
2 tbs. nonfat, light or regular sour cream
1 tbs. grated Parmesan cheese
1-2 tbs. water
½ tsp. Worcestershire sauce
salt and pepper to taste

Heat oven to 375°. Cut off the pointed end of garlic bulb. Place garlic in a garlic roaster or on a large sheet of aluminum foil, drizzle with oil and cover or wrap tightly. Bake for 35 to 45 minutes, until garlic cloves are very soft. Cool garlic and remove garlic pulp from skins by squeezing at base of bulb.

Place roasted garlic pulp, 3 tbs. olive oil, balsamic vinegar, white vinegar, sour cream, Parmesan, water, Worcestershire, salt and pepper in a blender container and blend until smooth. Makes 3/4 cup.

Serving suggestions: Serve on romaine, green leaf or red leaf lettuce. Toss with mushrooms, tomato, croutons and/or additional Parmesan cheese.

CREAMY-STYLE SALAD DRESSINGS

19

BLUE CHEESE-TARRAGON DRESSING

A salad tossed with this dressing needs few adornments. It is perfect tossed with ½ cup red seedless grapes: cut the grapes in half and toss them with the lettuce and dressing. The color will brighten up any dinner table.

1 cup olive oil
¼–⅓ cup seasoned rice vinegar
1¼ tsp. dried tarragon
½ tsp. Dijon-style mustard
¼ tsp. finely minced garlic
3 oz. blue cheese, crumbled

Combine all ingredients in a jar and shake vigorously until smooth. Chill for at least 1 hour to blend flavors. Makes 1½ cups.

CREAMY-STYLE SALAD DRESSINGS

Serving suggestions: Serve on red leaf or butter lettuce. Toss with avocado and walnuts or pine nuts.

Create an appetizer: Fresh Fruit with Blue Cheese and Tarragon

Drizzle dressing over a plate of sliced pears and apples.

Create an entrée: Chicken, Grape and Walnut Salad

Cut cooked chicken into bite-sized pieces and mix with dressing to taste. Add halved red grapes, walnut pieces and chopped celery to taste and mix thoroughly. Serve on a bed of lettuce or between slices of fresh bread.

CREAMY FETA DRESSING

This fairly thick dressing has a zesty Greek flavor. If you prefer a thinner consistency, add 1 to 2 tbs. water. Try it on calamari!

½ cup crumbled feta cheese
½–¾ cup canola or
   vegetable oil
¼ cup white wine vinegar
2 tbs. balsamic vinegar

1 tbs. sugar
1 tsp. dried parsley flakes
¼ tsp. pepper
⅛ tsp. salt

Process all ingredients with a blender or food processor until very smooth. Makes 1½ cups.

Serving suggestions: Serve on red leaf or romaine lettuce. Toss with kalamata olives, cucumber, tomato, red onion and additional crumbled feta cheese.

SMOKED MOZZARELLA DRESSING

This dressing is for smoked cheese lovers.

1/2–3/4 cup diced smoked
    mozzarella cheese
1/2 cup olive oil
1/4 cup balsamic vinegar
1/4 cup white wine vinegar

1 tbs. lemon juice
1/2 tsp. dried oregano
1/2 tsp. dried thyme
1/4 tsp. salt
1/4 tsp. pepper

Process all ingredients with a blender or food processor until smooth. Makes 1 1/2 cups.

Serving suggestions: Serve on romaine, green leaf or red leaf lettuce. Toss with tomato, mushrooms and/or croutons.

MISO DRESSING

The flavors in this dressing are reminiscent of those at a Japanese restaurant. Miso, or fermented soybean paste, is a common ingredient in Japanese cookery. Look for the soup mix in the international foods aisle, next to the soy sauce and other Japanese foods.

1 pkg. (.35 oz.) tofu miso soup mix

¼ cup warm water

2 tbs. seasoned rice vinegar

2 tbs. vegetable or canola oil

2 tbs. white wine vinegar

½ tbs. nonfat or light mayonnaise

1½ tsp. sugar

Combine all ingredients in a jar and shake vigorously until smooth. Makes ½-¾ cup.

Serving suggestions: Serve on finely chopped green or red cabbage, iceberg lettuce or green leaf lettuce. Toss with green onion and toasted sesame seeds.

Create an entrée: Japanese-Style Seared Tuna Salad
Sear ahi tuna steaks in a hot pan or wok with a small amount of dressing and a dash of soy sauce. Remove from pan and slice thinly. Toss shredded cabbage with dressing, place on serving plates and top with tuna slices. Sprinkle with chopped green onion and/or sesame seeds.

Create a side dish: Miso-Laced Rice
Swirl dressing into hot cooked rice to taste.

CREAMY-STYLE SALAD DRESSINGS

THAI PEANUT DRESSING

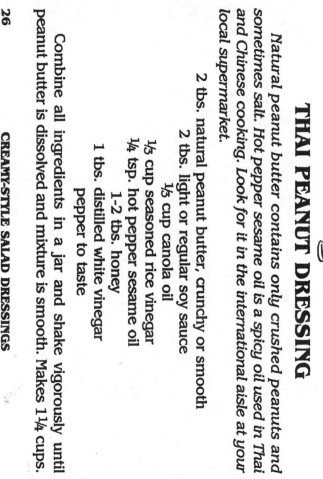

Natural peanut butter contains only crushed peanuts and sometimes salt. Hot pepper sesame oil is a spicy oil used in Thai and Chinese cooking. Look for it in the international aisle at your local supermarket.

2 tbs. natural peanut butter, crunchy or smooth
2 tbs. light or regular soy sauce
⅓ cup canola oil
⅓ cup seasoned rice vinegar
¼ tsp. hot pepper sesame oil
1-2 tbs. honey
1 tbs. distilled white vinegar
pepper to taste

Combine all ingredients in a jar and shake vigorously until peanut butter is dissolved and mixture is smooth. Makes 1¼ cups.

Serving suggestions: Serve on romaine, green leaf or red leaf lettuce, or on chopped cabbage. Toss with red bell pepper, snow peas, raw zucchini, cabbage, broccoli, chives, crunchy noodles, sesame seeds and/or peanuts.

Create a side dish: Thai Peanut Noodles or Vegetables
Warm dressing on the stovetop or in the microwave and mix into cooked whole-wheat noodles and/or sautéed vegetables.

Create an entrée: Thai Peanut Chicken
Sauté boneless chicken breast strips in a small amount of dressing until cooked through. Add chicken to tossed salad, or toss chicken with noodles or vegetables.

CLASSIC VINAIGRETTE

This versatile vinaigrette is an everyday standby. Adjust the mustard and garlic to taste.

¼ cup olive oil
3 tbs. vegetable oil
3 tbs. balsamic vinegar
3 tbs. distilled white vinegar

2-3 tbs. Dijon-style mustard
3 tbs. honey
½-1 clove garlic, finely minced

Combine all ingredients in a jar and shake until well mixed. Makes 1⅛ cups.

Serving suggestions: Serve on mixed greens or on romaine or red leaf lettuce. Toss with green onion, avocado, crumbled walnuts and blue cheese and/or leftover chicken cubes.

CITRUS VINAIGRETTE

This light dressing has a blend of refreshing flavors.

1/4 cup orange juice
3 tbs. white wine vinegar
2 tsp. fresh lemon juice
1/4 cup vegetable oil
2 tsp. sugar

1 tsp. Dijon-style mustard
1 tsp. grated fresh orange
  peel (zest)
1 clove garlic, finely minced
1/4 tsp. salt

Combine all ingredients in a jar and shake until well mixed. Makes 3/4 cup.

Serving suggestions: Serve on butter lettuce or spinach. Toss with carrot, jicama, avocado, green onion, orange slices and/or grapefruit slices.

LEMON-LIME VINAIGRETTE

If you like the tingly, tart sensation that you get when tasting lemons, you will like this dressing. It wakes up your whole mouth!

6 tbs. olive oil
2 tbs. fresh lemon juice
1 tbs. fresh lime juice
1 tsp. Dijon-style mustard

2 tsp. finely grated Parmesan
    cheese
1 tsp. freshly ground pepper
¼ tsp. salt

Place all ingredients in a jar and shake until well mixed. Makes ½ cup.

Serving suggestions: Serve on green leaf, romaine or butter lettuce, or on mixed greens. Toss with carrot, onion, beets, sprouts and/or mushrooms.

SOY-LEMON VINAIGRETTE

The mixture of lemon and soy is delightful.

½ cup vegetable or canola oil
¼ cup fresh lemon juice
2 tbs. light or regular soy sauce
1 tbs. white wine

2 tsp. grainy Dijon-style mustard
¼ tsp. finely minced garlic
freshly ground pepper to taste

Combine all ingredients in a jar and shake until well mixed. Makes 1 cup.

Serving suggestions: Serve on oak leaf, green leaf or romaine lettuce. Toss with snow peas, tomato, bean sprouts, grilled eggplant, toasted sesame seeds and/or peanuts.

Create an entrée: Sesame-Marinated Scallops
Marinate scallops in dressing before sautéing or grilling. Serve on dressed greens topped with sesame seeds.

MERLOT VINAIGRETTE

This delicate dressing won't overpower your greens. If you do not have Merlot, try Cabernet Sauvignon.

5½ tbs. Merlot wine
¼ cup red wine vinegar
⅓ cup canola or vegetable oil
1½ tsp. sugar
½ tsp. Dijon-style mustard
salt and pepper to taste

Combine all ingredients in a jar and shake until well mixed. Makes 1 cup.

Serving suggestions: Serve on oak leaf lettuce or mixed greens. Toss with carrot, red onion, Brie cheese and/or pecan pieces.

Create an appetizer: Mixed Greens with Brie, Pecans and Merlot Vinaigrette

Serve dressed greens on individual plates with slices of warm Brie cheese and small clumps of wine grapes or seedless red grapes. Sprinkle with pecan pieces.

CHINESE-STYLE SALAD DRESSING

This dressing originated from a desire to duplicate a favorite salad from a local restaurant. The creative process was tedious, but it was well worth it. I think that you will agree!

½ cup safflower or canola oil
½ cup seasoned rice vinegar*
½ tbs. sugar
¼ tsp. finely minced garlic
¼ tsp. salt
¼-½ tsp. freshly ground pepper

Combine all ingredients in a jar and shake until well mixed. Makes 1 cup.

* If using unseasoned rice vinegar, increase sugar to 2 tbs.

Serving suggestions: Serve on strips of green leaf and iceberg lettuce. Toss with green onion, red bell pepper, crunchy Chinese noodles, Mandarin orange slices and/or toasted sesame seeds.

Create an entrée: Chinese Chicken Salad

Pound chicken breasts until thin and cut into strips. Sauté strips in a small amount of dressing and a dash of peanut oil, if desired. Cool and toss with dressed salad greens and desired garnishes.

TOASTED SESAME VINAIGRETTE

Although toasting the sesame seeds takes an extra few moments, it is worth it for the added flavor. Try this dressing on sliced cooked chicken.

1 tbs. sesame seeds
1/4 cup canola or vegetable oil
2 tbs. seasoned rice vinegar
1 tbs. distilled white vinegar
2 tsp. light or regular soy sauce
1/2–3/4 tsp. grated fresh ginger

Heat broiler. Spread sesame seeds on a nonstick baking sheet and broil until browned, watching constantly. Add to a blender container with remaining ingredients and process until well mixed. Makes 1/2 cup.

Serving suggestions: Serve on finely chopped iceberg and romaine lettuce, or on chopped mixed vegetables or cabbage. Toss with yellow or red bell pepper, green onion, chives and/or additional toasted sesame seeds.

Create an entrée: Grilled Sesame-Marinated Fish

Marinate mahi-mahi or other fish in a small amount of the dressing before grilling. Serve over cabbage or rice and top with additional dressing (do not use dressing that was used for marinating) and chopped cashews. You may need to double the dressing recipe.

HONEY-PEPPER VINAIGRETTE

Yes, you do use 4 tsp. pepper. Trust that the combination of ingredients works well to mellow and complement the pepper.

⅔ cup olive oil

⅓ cup grapeseed oil or canola oil

¼ cup honey, warmed

3 tbs. raspberry vinegar

3 tbs. balsamic vinegar

1 shallot, finely minced

2 cloves garlic, finely minced

4 tsp. freshly ground pepper

1 tsp. salt

Combine all ingredients in a jar and shake until well mixed. Makes 1½ cups.

Serving suggestions: Serve on green leaf, red leaf or romaine lettuce, or on mixed greens. Toss with corn kernels, mushrooms, tomato, fresh raspberries, sunflower kernels, pumpkin seeds and/or pine nuts.

THYME-HONEY VINAIGRETTE

This sweet, flavorful dressing is sure to be a hit. Chèvre (soft white goat cheese) and walnuts are an elegant addition to a salad coated with this dressing. Play with the quantity of honey to find a level of sweetness that suits you.

½ cup canola or vegetable oil
¼ cup cider vinegar
¼ cup fresh lemon juice
¼ cup honey
1-1½ tsp. dried thyme
salt and pepper to taste

Combine all ingredients in a jar and shake until well mixed. Makes 1 cup.

Serving suggestions: Serve on oak leaf or butter lettuce. Toss with red onion, warm chèvre cheese and/or walnuts.

VINAIGRETTES

39

MINT VINAIGRETTE

Invigorating mint makes a cool, crisp addition to salads.

¼ cup vegetable or canola oil	2 tbs. (heaping) chopped fresh
2 tbs. fresh lemon juice	mint leaves
2 tbs. distilled white vinegar	¼ tsp. salt
2 tbs. honey	freshly ground pepper to taste

Combine all ingredients in a jar and shake until well mixed. Chill for at least 1 hour to blend flavors. Makes ¾ cup.

Serving suggestions: Serve on oak leaf or butter lettuce, or on mixed greens. Toss with onion, cucumber, orange slices, slivered almonds and/or goat cheese.

Create an appetizer: Minty Fruit Salad

Drizzle dressing over fruit salad. Or, serve over alternating slices of apple, orange and pear; top with crumbled goat cheese.

FRESH BASIL-PARMESAN VINAIGRETTE

For the garlic lovers out there, use a large clove of garlic. Or, be daring and add another clove!

1/4–1/3 cup chopped fresh basil leaves
1/2–3/4 cup olive oil
1/3–1/2 cup finely grated Parmesan cheese

2 tbs. balsamic vinegar
2 tbs. white wine vinegar
1 small clove garlic, minced
1/4 tsp. freshly ground pepper
1/8 tsp. salt

Combine all ingredients in a jar and shake until well mixed. Chill for at least 2 hours to blend and mellow flavors. Makes 1 cup.

Serving suggestions: Serve on green leaf or romaine lettuce, or on exotic mixed greens. Toss with vine-ripened yellow or red cherry tomatoes and/or croutons.

PESTO VINAIGRETTE

Using prepared pesto sauce as your "starter" is a great way to save time.

¼ cup prepared or homemade pesto, well mixed
¼ cup white wine vinegar
1-2 tbs. lemon juice
pepper to taste

Combine all ingredients in a jar and shake until well mixed. Makes ½ cup.

Serving suggestions: Serve on romaine or green leaf lettuce. Toss with vine-ripened yellow or red tomato, croutons, mozzarella chunks and/or shaved hard cheese, such as Parmesan or Romano.

Create an appetizer: Tomato and Fresh Mozzarella Salad
On a platter, arrange alternating slices of vine-ripened tomatoes and fresh mozzarella cheese. Drizzle with dressing and garnish with fresh basil leaves.

Create an entrée: Pesto Pasta Salad
Toss dressing with cooled cooked pasta, halved cherry tomatoes and cubed mozzarella cheese. Garnish with fresh basil leaves.

CILANTRO-TOMATO VINAIGRETTE

For a great Mexican fiesta, serve this dressing on a salad to accompany burritos, tacos or stuffed chile peppers.

1½ cups diced seeded fresh tomatoes
½ cup canola or vegetable oil
½ cup cilantro leaves, loosely packed
¼ cup white wine vinegar
¾ tsp. granulated garlic
½ tsp. freshly ground pepper
¼ tsp. chili powder
juice from 1 lime
salt to taste

Process all ingredients with a blender or food processor until desired texture is achieved. Makes 1½ cups.

Serving suggestions: Serve on romaine or green leaf lettuce. Toss with corn kernels, green or red bell pepper, avocado, tomato and/or black beans.

Create an entrée: Southwestern-Style Chicken Salad

Cut leftover cooked chicken into strips and toss with dressed salad greens and garnishes. Or, place 1 grilled chicken breast on each serving of tossed salad and drizzle extra dressing over the top (this version works best when the dressing is left slightly chunky).

RED PEPPER-PARSLEY VINAIGRETTE

Red bell pepper pieces give this dressing a nice crunchy texture.

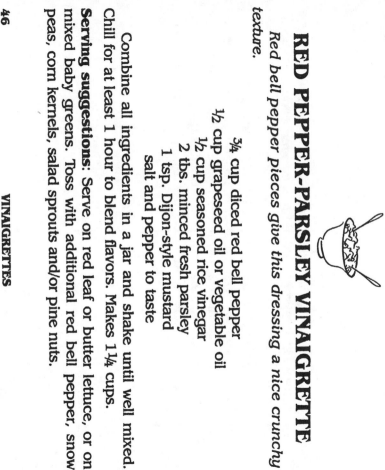

- 3/4 cup diced red bell pepper
- 1/2 cup grapeseed oil or vegetable oil
- 1/2 cup seasoned rice vinegar
- 2 tbs. minced fresh parsley
- 1 tsp. Dijon-style mustard
- salt and pepper to taste

Combine all ingredients in a jar and shake until well mixed. Chill for at least 1 hour to blend flavors. Makes 1¼ cups.

Serving suggestions: Serve on red leaf or butter lettuce, or on mixed baby greens. Toss with additional red bell pepper, snow peas, corn kernels, salad sprouts and/or pine nuts.

HERB-SCALLION VINAIGRETTE

This handy, all-purpose dressing works on any vegetables or greens that you happen to have in the house.

1/4 cup olive oil
2 tbs. red wine vinegar
2 tbs. distilled white vinegar
1 tbs. (heaping) finely chopped
   green onions (scallions)
1/4 tsp. dried oregano
1/4 tsp. dried thyme
1/4 tsp. dried basil
1/4 tsp. dried parsley
1/8 tsp. salt
freshly ground pepper to taste

Combine all ingredients in a jar and shake until well mixed. Use immediately, or let stand to develop flavors. Makes 1/2 cup.

Serving suggestions: Serve on romaine, green leaf or red leaf lettuce, or on mixed greens. Toss with mushrooms, tomato, green or red bell pepper, cucumber, sprouts, carrot, corn, garbanzo beans, blue cheese, feta cheese, croutons, pine nuts and/or pumpkin seeds.

WILD MUSHROOM VINAIGRETTE

This dressing has a nice earthy flavor. Use porcini, portobello or a combination of different dried mushrooms.

1 tbs. coarsely chopped shallot
¼ cup balsamic vinegar
1 pkg. (.35 oz.) dried mushrooms
about 2 cups boiling water
1 tbs. distilled white vinegar
1 tbs. sherry
½ tsp. dried thyme
pepper to taste
⅓ cup olive oil

Place shallot in a bowl with balsamic vinegar and let stand while preparing remaining ingredients.

Place mushrooms in a heatproof bowl with boiling water and let stand for about 2-5 minutes. Drain mushrooms, reserving soaking liquid.

In a blender container, combine mushrooms, 1 to 2 tbs. of the soaking liquid, shallot-vinegar mixture, white vinegar, sherry, thyme and pepper. With machine running, gradually add olive oil and process until almost smooth. If mixture seems too thick, add additional mushroom soaking liquid and process until desired consistency is achieved. Makes 3/4-1 cup.

Serving suggestions: Serve on mixed greens or spinach. Toss with sautéed, roasted or raw mushrooms and Parmesan cheese.

Create an appetizer: Portobello Mushroom Salad
Drizzle dressing over a cluster of sautéed portobello mushroom strips and top with shaved Parmesan cheese.

SAGE-LEEK VINAIGRETTE

The unique, woodsy flavor of this dressing makes it a great change of pace from the ordinary choices.

¾ cup canola oil
¼-⅓ cup white wine vinegar
12-15 leaves fresh sage
½ cup chopped leeks, white part only
2 tbs. sherry

½ tsp. grainy Dijon-style mustard
¼ tsp. dried parsley flakes
¼ tsp. salt
freshly ground pepper to taste

Process all ingredients with a blender until almost smooth. Makes 1¼ cups.

Serving suggestions: Serve on mixed exotic greens or on green leaf or red leaf lettuce. Toss with porcini, shiitake and/or brown mushrooms, sprouts, finely chopped grilled chicken and/or croutons.

ROASTED ONION VINAIGRETTE

The rich, caramelized onion flavor adds depth to salads. Or, try it drizzled over roasted vegetables.

1 medium-sized red onion
1/4 cup olive oil, plus more for drizzling
1/4 cup balsamic vinegar, plus more for drizzling
1 tbs. lemon juice
1 tsp. brown sugar
1/4 tsp. freshly ground pepper
1/8 tsp. salt
1-2 tbs. water, optional

Heat oven to 400°. Place onion on a large sheet of aluminum foil and drizzle with oil and vinegar. Roast for 45 to 60 minutes, until soft. Peel onion and process with a blender or food processor with remaining ingredients, except water, until smooth. Thin with water until desired consistency is achieved. Makes 1 cup.

Serving suggestions: Serve on mixed baby greens or spinach. Toss with cooked mushrooms and bacon pieces.

SHALLOT VINAIGRETTE

This all-purpose vinaigrette keeps well in the refrigerator for up to 2 weeks.

⅓ cup vegetable or canola oil
¼ cup red wine vinegar
1 tbs. minced shallot
1 tbs. fresh lemon juice
½ tsp. Worcestershire sauce

½ tsp. dry mustard
½ tsp. freshly ground pepper
¼ tsp. salt
¼ tsp. granulated garlic

Combine all ingredients in a jar and shake until well mixed. Serve immediately, or let stand for about 1 hour to blend flavors. Makes ⅔ cup.

Serving suggestions: Serve on romaine or red leaf lettuce, or on mixed greens. Toss with tomato, mushrooms, carrot, beans, sprouts, croutons and/or blue, Parmesan or feta cheese.

RASPBERRY VINAIGRETTE

This light and luscious dressing has beautiful color. Look for Dole Country Raspberry Juice in a carton with the refrigerated orange juice. You might also find concentrated, canned raspberry juice in the frozen food section at the supermarket.

3/4-1 cup grapeseed oil or vegetable oil
1/4 cup raspberry juice
1/4 cup raspberry vinegar
2-3 tbs. fresh lemon juice
1 tbs. honey

Process all ingredients with a blender on the "stir" setting until well mixed. Makes 1¾ cups.

Serving suggestions: Serve on red leaf, oak leaf or butter lettuce. Toss with jicama, petite peas, avocado, fresh raspberries and/or sunflower kernels.

PAPAYA VINAIGRETTE

This subtle, mild vinaigrette is a good choice when you are in the mood for a light salad. Papaya juice is sometimes difficult to find. You might find it in 12-ounce cans labeled as "papaya nectar."

3/4 cup canned papaya juice	1/4 tsp. ground ginger
1/2 cup vegetable or grape seed oil	1/4 tsp. celery seeds
	1/2 tsp. salt
1/3 cup cider vinegar	1/4 tsp. pepper

Combine all ingredients in a jar and shake until well mixed. Chill for 1 hour to blend flavors. Makes 1½ cups.

Serving suggestions: Serve on oak leaf or butter lettuce. Toss with celery, avocado, fresh papaya and/or sprouts.

DRIED CRANBERRY VINAIGRETTE

To highlight the beautiful red color of this dressing, add additional dried cranberries to your salad. Their chewy texture contrasts nicely with the softer cranberries in the dressing.

½ cup grapeseed oil or
   canola oil
¼ cup apple cider vinegar
2 tbs. seasoned rice vinegar

1 tsp. sugar
½ tsp. dried tarragon
salt to taste
¼ cup dried cranberries

Combine oil, vinegars, sugar, tarragon and salt in a jar and shake until well mixed. Add cranberries and shake again. Chill for at least 30 minutes to soften cranberries. Makes 1¼ cups.

Serving suggestions: Serve on butter lettuce. Toss with crumbled Roquefort cheese and chopped toasted almonds.

DRIED CHERRY VINAIGRETTE

For a delicious salad, heat the dressing on the stovetop or in the microwave until warm and toss immediately with fresh spinach. The warm dressing wilts the spinach, creating a wonderful texture and richness. Top the salad with dollops of chèvre (soft white goat cheese) and a few slices of red onion.

½ cup chopped dried cherries
3 tbs. plus ¼ cup red wine vinegar
1 tbs. plus ½ cup olive oil
1 tbs. brown sugar
1 tsp. ground ginger
1 tbs. lemon juice
salt and pepper to taste

In a skillet over medium heat, sauté cherries, 3 tbs. vinegar and 1 tbs. olive oil until softened. Add brown sugar and ginger and stir over low heat until thickened.

Transfer mixture in skillet to a food processor workbowl or blender container. Add ¼ cup red wine vinegar and lemon juice. With machine running, gradually add ½ cup olive oil and process until well mixed. Season with salt and pepper. Makes ¾ cup.

Serving suggestions: Serve on fresh spinach. Toss with red onion and/or soft goat cheese.

Create an entrée: Grilled Duck or Pork with Cherry Sauce
Serve mixture from skillet as a sauce for grilled duck or pork. You may need to double the ingredients.

DRIED PEAR VINAIGRETTE

Tossed with mixed greens, sliced pear and crumbled blue-veined cheese, this dressing makes quite an elegant salad.

½ cup chopped dried pears	1 tbs. orange juice
½ cup canola oil	½ tbs. sugar
¼ cup white wine vinegar	¼-½ tsp. pepper
¼ cup cider vinegar	¼ tsp. salt
3 tbs. sweet wine, such as white Zinfandel or Riesling	1 tbs. water, optional

Process all ingredients, except water, with a food processor or blender until almost smooth. If dressing seems thick, add water and process until blended. Makes 1½ cups.

Serving suggestions: Serve on mixed baby greens or field greens, or on red leaf or oak leaf lettuce. Toss with blue cheese, Gorgonzola cheese or cambazola cheese, and/or sliced fresh pear.

Create an appetizer: Pear and Blue Cheese Salad

Toss greens with dressing and arrange on a salad plate. Place a fan of sliced pear (red pear adds nice color) next to greens. Top pear with crumbled or sliced blue-veined cheese.

MAPLE VINAIGRETTE

This dressing is so easy to make! Using maple syrup as a sweetener makes a subtle difference in this dressings.

> 3 tbs. pure maple syrup, warmed
> 3-4 tbs. white wine vinegar
> ¼ cup canola or vegetable oil
> 2 tbs. lemon juice

Combine all ingredients in a jar and shake until well mixed. Makes ¾ cup.

Serving suggestions: Serve on mixed baby greens, or on oak leaf or butter lettuce. Toss with dried currants, blue cheese and/or toasted walnuts or pecans, or *Sugared Pecans*, page 65.

CINNAMON-SPICE VINAIGRETTE

The unexpected blend of ingredients in this vinaigrette offers a nice change from the flavors that are usually associated with salads. This is a great salad dressing for the winter holdiay months.

¼ cup canola oil	½ tsp. cinnamon
6 tbs. red wine vinegar	½ tsp. pepper
2 tbs. honey	¼ tsp. salt
½ tsp. ground allspice	

Combine all ingredients in a jar and shake until well mixed. Use immediately or chill for 1 hour to blend flavors. Makes ⅔ cup.

Serving suggestions: Serve on warm or cold fresh spinach or mixed baby greens. Or, serve on oak leaf or red leaf lettuce. Toss with nuts and/or cheese, such as Brie, chèvre, blue or Gorgonzola.

FIG VINAIGRETTE

This salad truly tastes like something you would order in a fine restaurant. The texture of the figs goes well on a salad tossed with Sugared Pecans and goat cheese.

½ cup chopped dried figs
⅓ cup canola oil
¼ cup cider vinegar
2 tbs. distilled white vinegar
2 tbs. fresh lemon juice
2 tbs. honey

Combine all ingredients in a jar and shake until well mixed. Serve immediately or chill for at least 1 hour to blend flavors; flavors will intensify over time. Makes ¾-1 cup.

Serving suggestions: Serve on spinach, red leaf or oak leaf lettuce, or on mixed field greens. Toss with goat cheese and/or Sugared Pecans.

SUGARED PECANS

These crunchy, sweetened nuts are an added treat in a variety of salads.

2 cups pecans or walnuts
1 egg white, slightly beaten, or 2 tbs. butter, melted
2 tbs. brown sugar
dash cinnamon

Heat broiler. In a bowl, toss nuts with egg white or butter. Add brown sugar and cinnamon and toss well. Transfer coated nuts to a baking sheet and broil until bubbly, about 2 minutes. With a spatula, flip nuts and broil until bubbly, about 2 minutes. Cool before using. Makes 2 cups.

CRYSTALLIZED GINGER VINAIGRETTE

Try this sweet dressing on a chopped vegetable salad. You can buy prechopped bags of vegetables for ease.

½ cup chopped crystallized ginger

½ cup vegetable oil

2 tbs. seasoned rice vinegar

2 tbs. fresh lemon juice

2-3 tbs. white vinegar

½ tsp. regular or light soy sauce

Process all ingredients with a food processor for 3 to 4 minutes, until ginger is chopped into fine bits. Makes 1 cup.

Serving suggestions: Serve on chopped iceberg and green leaf lettuce, or on shredded green cabbage. Toss with carrot, cauliflower, broccoli and/or cashew pieces.

Create a side dish: Quick Vegetable Slaw

Toss prepared chopped vegetables with dressing and cashew pieces to taste.

WALNUT VINAIGRETTE

Walnut oil has a tendency to become rancid quickly; it is important to smell your oil before using it. Always keep opened containers of walnut oil in the refrigerator, and consider buying it in small quantities.

¼ cup canola oil
2 tbs. walnut oil
3 tbs. distilled white vinegar
1-2 tbs. cider vinegar

1½ tbs. honey
¼ tsp. freshly ground pepper
⅛ tsp. salt
3 tbs. chopped walnuts

Combine all ingredients in a jar and shake until well mixed. Chill for at least 1 hour to blend flavors. Makes ¾ cup.

Serving suggestions: Serve on red leaf or oak leaf lettuce, or on mixed greens. Toss with dried currants or dried cranberries and/or crumbled blue or Gorgonzola cheese.

WARM TURKEY BACON DRESSING

Remember the old-fashioned warm bacon dressing that used to garnish spinach salads on restaurant menus? Here is a modern alternative. Substituting turkey bacon for regular bacon leaves out much of the fat without compromising flavor.

½ cup chopped cooked turkey bacon (about 5 slices)
¼ cup chopped sweet onion
¼ cup vegetable oil
¼ cup cider vinegar
1 tbs. distilled white vinegar
1 tbs. honey
2 tsp. Dijon-style mustard
¼ tsp. salt
freshly ground pepper to taste

Process all ingredients with a food processor or blender until well mixed. Makes 3/4-1 cup.

Serving suggestions: Serve warm on fresh spinach. Toss with avocado, extra pieces of cooked turkey bacon, hard-cooked eggs and/or croutons.

Create a side dish: Warm Spinach and Turkey Bacon Salad
Place dressing in an uncovered jar or pitcher. Heat in the microwave on HIGH for 20 to 40 seconds. Toss with spinach and croutons. Garnish with extra turkey bacon and hard-cooked eggs.

SMOKED TROUT VINAIGRETTE

Your guests will be surprised by the smoky treat that tops their salad. Smoked trout can be found in most grocery stores. Look for it in the fish department or in the deli near the smoked salmon.

¼ cup chopped boneless smoked trout

¼ cup olive oil

2 tbs. white wine vinegar

2 tbs. balsamic vinegar

freshly ground pepper to taste

Process all ingredients with a blender or food processor until fairly smooth. Makes ½ cup.

Serving suggestions: Serve on mixed field greens or red leaf lettuce. Toss with tomato, soft goat cheese (chèvre) and/or additional pieces of smoked trout.

Create an appetizer: Smoked Trout and Goat Cheese Salad

Toss greens with dressing and divide among individual salad plates. Arrange halved cherry tomatoes cut-side down in a circle around the edge of plates. Place about 1 tsp. goat cheese in the center of each plate and top cheese with 2 slices of smoked trout in an X pattern.

FAT-FREE ARTICHOKE DRESSING

Even though the color of this dressing may be lacking in appeal, the flavor makes up for it. The artichoke hearts thicken the dressing, eliminating the need for oil. They also lend a savory flavor and wonderful texture. The optional anchovy paste will add just a trace of fat. If this dressing is too tangy for you, replace 1 tbs. of the white vinegar with water.

1 cup drained canned artichoke hearts
   or crowns (water-packed)
¼ cup balsamic vinegar
2 tbs. distilled white vinegar

6-7 tbs. water
1½ tsp. dried parsley
¼ tsp. garlic powder
salt and freshly ground pepper to taste
1 tsp. anchovy paste, optional

FAT-FREE DRESSINGS

Chop artichokes and place in a blender container or food processor workbowl with balsamic vinegar, white vinegar, 3 tbs. of the water, parsley, garlic powder, salt and pepper and anchovy paste, if using. Process until smooth. Gradually blend in enough of the remaining water until dressing is thin enough to pour. Makes 1½ cups.

Serving suggestions: Serve on romaine or green leaf lettuce. Toss with onion, tomato and/or fat-free croutons.

FAT-FREE BALSAMIC-APPLE VINAIGRETTE

Apple gives this dressing a nice consistency without using any oil. Use any type of apple that isn't too tart.

⅓ cup balsamic vinegar
⅓ cup (heaping) chopped, peeled apple
1 clove garlic, crushed

½ tbs. Dijon-style mustard
½ tbs. honey
¼ tsp. freshly ground pepper
⅛ tsp. salt

Process all ingredients with a blender or food processor until almost smooth. Makes ½ cup.

Serving suggestions: Serve on mixed baby or exotic greens, or on red leaf lettuce. Toss with mushrooms, corn kernels, onion, fat-free croutons and/or sliced or chopped apple. Sprinkle with nuts or grated cheeses.*

* These items will add a small amount of fat.

FAT-FREE
HONEY-MUSTARD-BASIL DRESSING

Here's a new option for those who are trying to find light alternatives to high-fat salad dressings. You won't miss the oil!

5 tbs. balsamic vinegar	1 tbs. distilled white vinegar
2-3 tbs. chopped fresh basil	1 tbs. water
2 tbs. honey	¼ tsp. garlic salt
1½-2 tbs. Dijon-style mustard	freshly ground pepper to taste

Combine all ingredients in a jar and shake until well mixed. Chill for at least 1 hour to blend flavors. Makes ¾ cup.

Serving suggestions: Serve on mixed greens, spinach or red leaf lettuce. Toss with tomato, carrot, mushrooms and/or kidney beans. Sprinkle with sunflower kernels*.

* These items will add a small amount of fat.

FAT-FREE GREEN GODDESS DRESSING

Use this dressing to increase your daily protein intake.

¼ cup chopped green onion
2 tbs. lemon juice
2 tbs. white wine vinegar
1 tbs. Dijon-style mustard
1 tbs. chopped fresh parsley

1 clove garlic, crushed
¼ tsp. salt
¼-½ tsp. freshly ground
   pepper
6 tbs. nonfat cottage cheese

Combine all ingredients, except cottage cheese, in a blender container. With machine running, gradually add cottage cheese and blend until smooth. Makes ⅔ cup.

Serving suggestions: Serve on green leaf or romaine lettuce. Toss with tomato, carrot, cucumber, onion, mushrooms, sprouts and/or fat-free croutons. Sprinkle with sunflower kernels or pumpkin seeds*.

* These items will add a small amount of fat.

FAT-FREE
STRAWBERRY-POPPY SEED DRESSING

This bright, slightly sweet dressing is cool and refreshing and has a lovely blush color. If you like a tangier dressing, eliminate the sugar. Use fresh or thawed frozen strawberries.

1/3 cup chopped strawberries
3 tbs. orange juice
2 tbs. cider vinegar

1 tbs. fat-free mayonnaise
1/2 tsp. poppy seeds
1/2-1 tsp. sugar

Combine all ingredients in a jar and shake vigorously until well mixed. Makes 2/3 cup.

Serving suggestions: Serve on spinach or mixed baby greens, or on oak leaf or red leaf lettuce. Toss with extra sliced strawberries or orange or grapefruit slices. Or, use dressing to coat a fresh fruit salad.